D O - I T - Y O U R S E L F

ESSENTIAL TOOLS

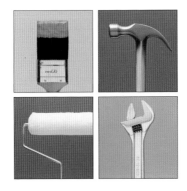

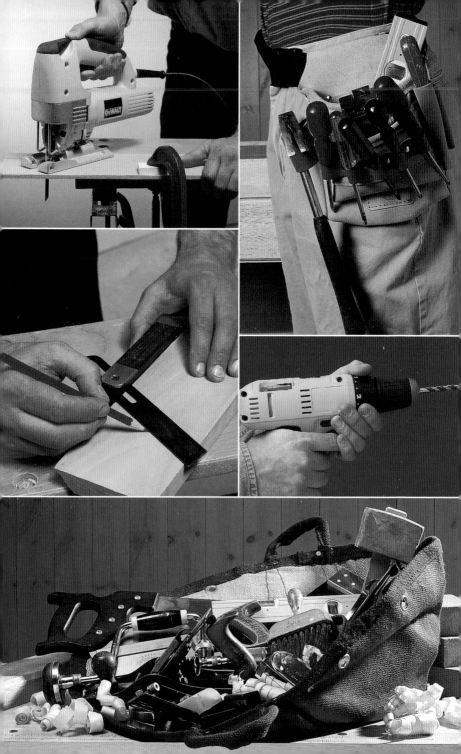

DO - IT - YOURSELF

ESSENTIAL
TOOLS

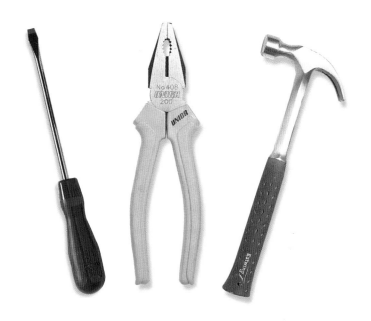

Mike Collins

LORENZ BOOKS

This edition is published by Lorenz Books,
an imprint of Anness Publishing Ltd,
Blaby Road,
Wigston,
Leicestershire LE18 4SE;

info@anness.com

www.lorenzbooks.com;
www.annesspublishing.com

If you like the images in this book and
would like to investigate using them for
publishing, promotions or advertising,
please visit our website
www.practicalpictures.com for more
information.

Publisher: Joanna Lorenz
Editors: Felicity Forster, Anne Hildyard
Photographer: John Freeman
Illustrator: Andrew Green
Designer: Bill Mason
Production Controller: Pirong Wang

Additional text: Brenda Legge & Diane Carr

ACKNOWLEDGEMENTS AND NOTES
The publisher would like to
thank The Tool Shop for supplying
tools for jacket photography:
97 Lower Marsh
Waterloo, London SE1 7AB
Tel 020 7207 2077; Fax 020 7207 5222
www.thetoolshop-diy.com

The author and publishers have made
every effort to ensure that all instructions
contained within this book are accurate
and safe, and cannot accept liability for
any resulting injury, damage or loss to
persons or property, however it may arise.
If in any doubt as to the correct procedure
to follow for any home improvements
task, seek professional advice.

CONTENTS

INTRODUCTION

Most people have a few basic tools in their home: a hammer, a screwdriver or two, perhaps a saw of some sort and a couple of paintbrushes – just about enough to tackle the occasional simple job or essential temporary repair. The more competent are likely to have a more comprehensive basic tool kit containing such items as a retractable tape measure, a craft knife, adjustable spanner, hand and tenon saws, a spirit (carpenter's) level, screwdrivers for different types of screw head, perhaps a chisel or two, pliers, pincers, an electric drill and a variety of decorating tools.

ABOVE: A power drill makes drilling easy. Buy one that offers a choice of speeds, has a chuck capacity of at least 12mm (½in), and a hammer facility if you intend drilling masonry.

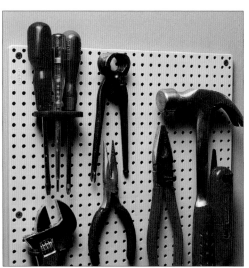

ABOVE: Mounting your tools on a perforated tool board is a good idea. You will be able to find what you need quickly, and it will be obvious when a tool is missing. Buy one or make your own.

Some people, of course, are determined do-it-yourselfers who gain much pleasure and satisfaction from doing as many jobs as they can around the home. Others may even have a practical hobby, such as woodwork or model-making, that requires a dedicated home workshop containing a variety of complex and versatile machinery together with a range of specialized hand tools.

Whatever your level of interest in do-it-yourself, choosing the right tools for each job you tackle is essential. Attempting any task without the proper tools is a recipe for disaster.

ABOVE: Of all the do-it-yourself tasks, decorating is probably the most common. Painting requires brushes and rollers; papering requires tools such as scissors, a pasting brush and a seam roller.

Most tool kits grow organically as specific tools are added when the need arises. The tools featured in this book show a useful selection for starting your own projects.

LEFT: A belt sander is useful for heavy-duty shaping and sanding. As well as being hand-held, it can be inverted and secured in a woodworking vice.

When buying tools, always go for the best you can afford; the adage, "You get what you pay for," is particularly appropriate. Cheap tools may bend or break and are unlikely to last long; good-quality tools will last you a lifetime. If your budget is tight, it is best to buy several hand tools rather than one power tool. This has the benefit of improving your manual skills at an early stage, which will give encouraging results as well as increase the range of jobs you can undertake.

USING PROFESSIONALS

As a do-it-yourself enthusiast, you have to be familiar with several trades, but it is often well worth employing a professional for structural work to save time and possibly money. There are many jobs, especially in plumbing and electrics, where professional help is welcome and indeed necessary. Professionals can also advise you in advance if your project is likely to fail for a reason you may not even have considered.

SAFETY & PREPARATION

Even the simplest of do-it-yourself jobs carries with it some degree of risk, if only from the danger of upsetting a can of paint. Some tasks, however, have the potential to cause serious injury, so safety should be uppermost in your mind at all times. You must use the proper tools in the correct manner, wear appropriate clothing, ensure you have safe access to the job and take steps to protect others who may be at risk. Storing your tools correctly is important, too. Not only will they be ready for use when you need them, but they will also be protected from damage and from damaging other tools. Completing any do-it-yourself task can be immensely satisfying; the following pages show you how to do so in complete safety.

AWARENESS AND CLOTHING

A complete book could be devoted to the subject of safety in the home, and there is a wide range of equipment designed to minimize our capacity for hurting ourselves. Nevertheless, there is one requirement that we cannot buy, without which all that equipment is virtually useless, namely concentration. This is particularly important when working alone.

ABOVE: Wear overalls to protect your clothes when painting, decorating or carrying out any dirty or dusty job. Disposable types are available for one-off jobs.

AWARENESS

Concentration is essential when using any form of power tool, especially a saw, where one slip can mean the loss of a finger, or worse. The dangers of accidents involving electricity are well documented, as are those involving falls from ladders, spillages of toxic materials, and burns and injuries caused by contact with fire or abrasive surfaces. In almost every case, there is a loss of concentration, coupled with poor work practices and inadequate protective clothing or equipment. So, although the items shown here are all useful, concentrating on what you are doing is the best advice to prevent accidents from occurring.

CLOTHING

Overalls are a good investment because they not only protect clothing, but are also designed to be close-fitting to prevent accidental contact with moving machinery. Industrial gloves provide protection against cuts and bruises when doing rough jobs, such as fencing and garden work. Safety boots should be worn when lifting heavy objects or when the use of machinery is involved.

Knee pads are necessary for comfort when carrying out any job that requires a lot of kneeling. They will also protect the wearer from injury if a nail or similar projection is knelt on accidentally. Finally, a bump cap will protect the head from minor injuries, but is not so cumbersome as the hard hat required on building sites.

ABOVE: A pair of thick gloves will be essential when handling rough materials such as sawn wood or sharp objects such as broken glass. Make sure they fit well.

ABOVE: If you have to do a job that involves a lot of kneeling, rubber knee pads will be invaluable. They provide comfort and protection from sharp projections such as nail heads.

ABOVE: Safety boots with steel toe caps will protect your feet from injury when working with heavy items such as large sections of wood, bricks and concrete blocks.

ABOVE: When working in situations where you may hit your head accidentally, the bump cap will provide protection without being as cumbersome as a conventional hard hat.

SAFETY EQUIPMENT

Make sure you have the appropriate safety equipment to hand when carrying out do-it-yourself tasks, and always use it. Doing so can prevent nasty accidents and serious injury.

AIRBORNE DANGERS

When you are working with wood, the most common airborne danger is dust, mainly from sawing and sanding. This can do long-term damage to the lungs. Many do-it-yourself enthusiasts do not do enough work to warrant a workshop dust extractor, but it would be worth considering if funds allowed. Such a

BELOW: Typical personal safety equipment – first aid kit, impact-resistant safety spectacles, ear protectors, two types of dust mask and sturdy industrial-type gloves.

KEEPING IN TOUCH

Perhaps the most basic advice is never to work alone with machinery and, if it is possible, always have a friend or colleague nearby to help. If there is no telephone, having a mobile (cell) phone in the workshop is useful.

device can be wall-mounted or portable. In the latter case, it can be moved around the house or workshop to suit any tool in use.

A simple face mask, however, will offer adequate protection for occasional jobs. These can also be purchased for protection against fumes, such as from solvents, which can be very harmful. Dust, of course,

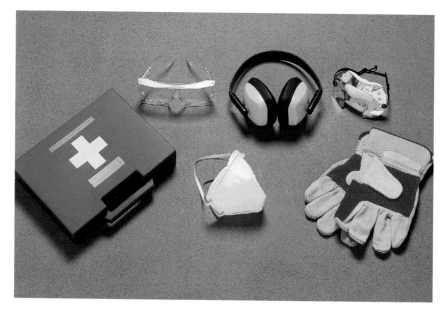

also affects the eyes, so it is worth investing in a pair of impact-resistant goggles, which will protect the wearer from both fine dust and flying debris. Full facial protection is available as a powered respirator for those working in dusty conditions over long periods.

Excessive noise is another airborne pollutant that can be dangerous over a long period. Power tools, particularly woodworking machinery such as planers and circular saws, are major culprits. Earplugs are the simplest solution and can be left in the ears over a long period. If you need to be able to hear between short bouts of working, ear protectors are the answer. These can be worn in conjunction with other facial protection quite easily.

FIRST AID

Keeping a basic first aid kit is a common and wise precaution even before any do-it-yourself work is envisaged. It should always be prominently displayed for people unfamiliar with your workshop.

You can buy a home first aid kit that will contain all the necessary items to cope with minor injuries, or you can assemble your own, keeping it in a plastic sandwich box with an airtight lid, which should be clearly marked. You should include items such as bandages, plasters, wound dressings, antiseptic cream, eye pads, scissors, tweezers and pins. If you have cause to use the kit, replace the items you have removed as soon as possible.

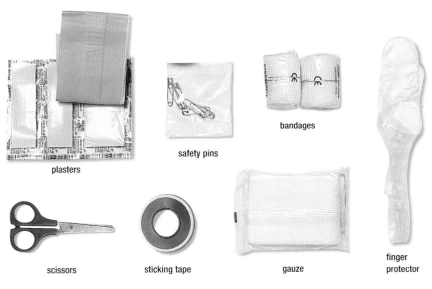

bandages

safety pins

plasters

scissors   sticking tape   gauze   finger protector

ABOVE: Some of the basic items found in a first aid kit.

ELECTRICAL AND FIRE SAFETY

If used incorrectly, the dangers of electrical equipment can be life threatening, and the dangers of fire are obvious. Always treat the former with respect, and take sensible precautions against the latter.

ELECTRICAL SAFETY

Some tools have removable switches that allow the user to immobilize them and prevent any unauthorized use. Provisions for the use of padlocks are also common on machinery, and it is wise to buy tools with such facilities.

To safeguard against electrocution, which can occur if the flex (power cord) is faulty or is cut accidentally, the ideal precaution is a residual current device (RCD). This is simply plugged into the main supply socket (electrical outlet) before the flex and will give complete protection to the user. Extension leads can be purchased with automatic safety cutouts and insulated sockets, and are ideal for outside and inside work.

The danger of electrocution or damage caused by accidentally drilling into an existing cable or pipe can be largely prevented by using an electronic pipe and cable detector, which will locate and differentiate between metal pipes, wooden studs and live wires through plaster and concrete to a depth of approximately 50mm (2in). These are not too expensive and will be very useful around the home.

FIRE SAFETY

The danger of fire is ever-present in both the home and workshop, so a fire extinguisher (possibly two or three) is necessary for every do-it-yourself enthusiast. It should be wall-mounted in plain view and serviced regularly.

LEFT: A simple circuit breaker can save a life by cutting off the power to faulty equipment.

ABOVE: A fire extinguisher is absolutely essential in the workshop or at home. Make sure the one you have is adequate for the size and type of your workshop, and the type of fire source.

LADDER SAFETY

Steps and ladders can be hazardous, so make sure they are in good condition. Accessories include a roof hook, which slips over the ridge for safety; a ladder stay, which spreads the weight of the ladder across a vertical surface, such as a wall, to prevent slippage; and a standing platform, which is used to provide a more comfortable and safer surface to stand on. The last often has a ribbed rubber surface and can be attached to the rungs of almost all ladders. Even more stable is a movable workstation or a board or staging slung between two pairs of steps or trestles. These can often be used with a safety rail, which prevents the operator from falling even if a slip occurs.

TIPS

- Never over-reach when working on steps or a ladder; climb down and reposition it.
- Never allow children or pets into areas where power tools or strong solvents are being used.
- Do not work when you are overtired. This causes lapses in concentration, which can lead to silly and/or dangerous mistakes being made.
- Keep the work environment tidy. Flexes (power cords) should not be walked on or coiled up tightly, because it damages them internally. Moreover, trailing flexes can be a trip hazard, and long extension leads can be prone to overheating.

ABOVE: A ladder platform will provide a firm footing, especially if heavy footwear is worn.

ABOVE: A movable workstation simplifies the process of working at a height.

ABOVE: Platforms supported by trestles offer a safe means of painting from a height.

WORKBENCHES AND VICES

A solid and stable surface is essential for producing good work, and serious thought should be given to this by the enthusiast. A good bench need not be too expensive, nor too pretty; the prime requirements are sturdy construction, a flat-top surface and at least one good vice somewhere on the front of the bench. You can make your own or buy one, but beware of cheap benches that may not be up to the job. Suppliers and auctions of used industrial equipment are good sources.

PORTABLE WORKBENCHES

By far the most popular form of portable support is the foldaway workbench. This is really convenient to use, both in the workshop, in the home and outdoors. It has the ingenious feature of a bench top constructed in two halves, which is capable of acting as a vice. It is handy for holding awkward shapes, such as pipes and large dowels.

VICES

Your main workshop vice should be heavy and sturdy. It is normally screwed to the bench, close to one of the legs. If you intend doing a lot of woodworking, buy one with a quick-release action that allows you to open and close the jaws quickly, using the handle for final adjustments. You should certainly be able to fit false wooden jaws to prevent damage to the material you are working with.

ABOVE: Lightweight plastic sawhorses can be useful if you are undertaking small jobs.

ABOVE: A portable foldaway workbench with adjustable bench top.

ABOVE: Wooden sawhorses come in pairs and are often home-made.

Additional ways of protecting the work in the vice take the form of magnetic vice jaws faced with cork, rubber or aluminium, which fit inside the main jaws of the steel bench vice.

Another useful and portable addition to the bench is the swivelling bench-top vice. This can be fitted easily and removed very quickly, usually by means of a screw clamp. It is particularly handy for holding small pieces of work in awkward positions, when carving, for example. However, it is too light in construction to support work that is to be struck with any force.

The mitre clamp can also be considered as a bench vice of sorts and is useful for holding any assemblies that require clamping at 45 degrees, such as picture and mirror frames. Good quality examples are made from metal, since plastic will tend to flex when pressure is applied.

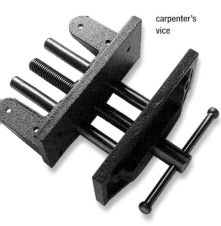

carpenter's vice

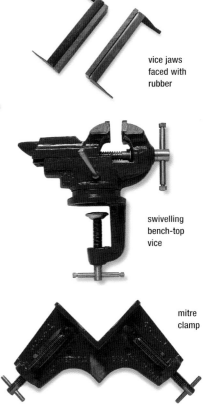

vice jaws faced with rubber

swivelling bench-top vice

mitre clamp

TIPS

• Spend time adjusting your workbench to the exact height that suits you. An incorrect height can prove to be very tiring and is not good for your back. Never shorten the legs of a bench if it is too high; work off a duckboard if necessary.
• Always buy the best-quality vice you can afford; second-hand ones can be particularly good value.

TOOL STORAGE

Tidy and effective storage of your tools pays off in many ways. Properly stored tools will be protected from the atmosphere and will not rust or discolour. The sharp cutting edges of saws and chisels will be protected from damage, as will the potential user's fingers. Moreover, tools will always be easily found near at hand when they are needed.

STORAGE

Efficient storage saves bench and floor space for other uses, and tools will be more easily located, saving time and frustration. It is well worth taking the trouble to devise and even make your own storage facilities. There are plenty of benches, cabinets, racks, clips and tool rolls on the market so that you can equip your workshop with exactly what you need. Remember, too, that storage for tools often needs to be portable, so tool pouches and carrying bags also need to be part of the overall picture.

metal toolbox

drill bit roll

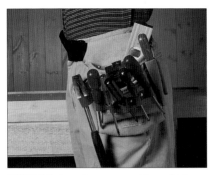

ABOVE: A tool pouch worn around the waist is ideal for carrying tools when working in different parts of the home.

PORTABLE STORAGE

The traditional carpenter's tool bag can still be obtained. Made from heavy canvas, it has two carrying handles and brass eyelets for closing.

Compact, compartmentalized plastic or metal toolboxes with drawers, carrying handles and safety locks are another option for carrying tools from one job to another.

A leather tool pouch can be worn around the waist and has loops and pockets for tools as well as screws and nails. Various sizes and styles are available. They are ideal for use on projects that require you to keep moving about.

Drill bits and chisels should always be carried in a tool roll with their tips covered for protection. Some chisels are provided with individual plastic blade caps, and many saws are sold with a plastic blade guard to protect the teeth when not in use. Always make sure that these are fitted correctly.

STATIC STORAGE

The most important static storage space is that below the workbench top, and often this takes the form of cabinets or drawers. A useful device is a large tilting drawer, which can easily be made and is ideal for storing tools that are in frequent use.

Wall-mounted cabinets with sliding doors are really practical in the workshop. The sliding doors allow them to be sited in confined areas and make it impossible to hit your head on them when they are open, which is especially important above the bench.

Shelving units come in a variety of materials, shapes and sizes, and most can be added to as the need arises.

The tool board has the advantage of not only displaying the tools, but also making it obvious when a tool has not been replaced. To make one, arrange the tools on a flat board and draw around them with a marker pen. Then fit hooks, pegs or clips as necessary.

ABOVE: Specifically made in transparent plastics for easy identification of the contents, storage drawers for screws, nails, clips and a host of other small items are a must.

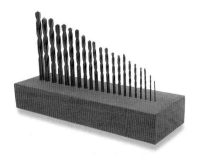

ABOVE: Use a length of wood to make your own storage block to keep your drill bits tidy.

MAKING A TOOL BOARD

When making a tool board, remember to leave space around each tool so that it can be lifted clear when the board is on the wall. Draw around the tools with a felt-tipped pen to indicate their positions. Hammer in nails or hooks that will hold them in place. Wall hooks will hold larger items, such as saws. Alternatively, you can buy a tool board made from perforated plywood from a local builder's merchant.

MEASURING, SHAPING & CUTTING

One of the most crucial skills for do-it-yourself work is the ability to measure accurately. The quality of much of the work you undertake will rely on that skill, so it is worth taking time and care when measuring and marking out. Shaping wood is a task required for many projects, and knowing how to use a plane will pay dividends. Chisels are also used for this purpose, as well as making cutouts. To be effective, both tools must be kept sharp. A good tool kit will also include a variety of saws and knives; make sure you know which to use and when. Drilling holes is something you will need to do on a regular basis, and there are many types of drill and drill bit to choose from.

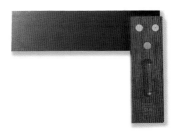

MEASURING TOOLS

Accurate measuring is a very basic, but essential, skill for the do-it-yourself enthusiast to master. Time spent on perfecting measuring is never wasted. The golden rule is to measure twice and cut once. Buy good-quality tools – poor measuring and marking devices can lose their accuracy very quickly and spoil your work.

HOW TO MEASURE

There are dozens of types of flat, rigid rule for marking out, most of which are calibrated in both metric and imperial units. They may be wood or steel, although some cheaper varieties are plastic. Where curves are involved, greater accuracy will be achieved with a flexible steel rule or even a retractable steel tape, which can be bent around the work.

The T-square is useful for marking out large sheets of manufactured board such as plywood, MDF (medium-density fiberboard) and blockboard. Remember, however, that it must be used on a perfectly straight edge to produce a 90-degree line across the sheet. Any small discrepancy in the edge will be greatly magnified across the sheet width and even more so along the length.

The combination square incorporates a number of functions in one tool, and is used for both measuring and marking out. It comprises a graduated steel rule that slides within a shaped body. A clamping screw permits the rule to be secured at any point along its length, while the body itself has flat edges that allow guidelines to be marked at 90 and 45 degrees to a straight surface. Many combination squares also feature a spirit bubble, allowing the tool to be used for checking horizontals.

FITTING PRE-MADE STRUCTURES

When fitting previously-assembled cabinets or shelving to a wall, the most accurate method is to mark out the wall using a spirit (carpenter's) level. These are available in long and short lengths. Do not rely on existing lines, such as architraves (trims) around doors, picture rails or skirtings (baseboards), as these may not be truly horizontal.

Transferring measurements from one point to another can also be done with a straightedge, and although this is very similar to a heavy steel rule, the bevelled edge gives it the added advantage of being very easy to cut or mark against. Straightedges often have handles, making them easy to hold in place.

CONVERTING MEASUREMENTS

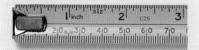

On small work in particular, never be tempted to convert from metric to imperial or vice versa. Some quite large errors can occur with standard conversions. Always work in the unit specified.

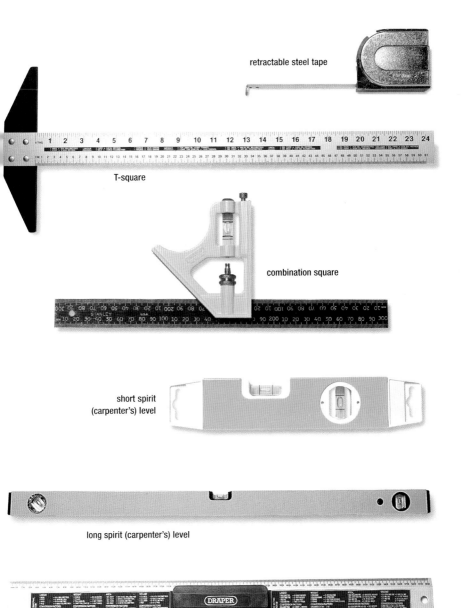

retractable steel tape

T-square

combination square

short spirit
(carpenter's) level

long spirit (carpenter's) level

straightedge

MARKING-OUT TOOLS

Another essential do-it-yourself skill is marking out, which can make or mar many projects.

Where you need to mark off a series of equal spacings, simply set a pair of dividers or callipers to the correct distance, using a flat wooden or steel rule, and step off the divisions.

You can mark out your workpiece for cutting and/or shaping with a pencil or a marking knife. The latter is particularly useful for fine work. An ordinary pencil is quite acceptable, but a flat carpenter's pencil will have a chisel-shaped tip when sharpened, making for more accurate marking.

MARKING JOINTS

Marking joints needs a fair degree of accuracy, so the first thing to ascertain is that your prepared wood is flat and square, which is done with a combination square or a try square. Either of these tools should be slid down the length of the wood to be cut, thus ensuring its uniformity and squareness.

For marking out a mortise, use a mortise gauge and set the points to the width of the chisel you intend to use to cut the mortise, not from a rule. This is far more accurate, as well as being much more convenient.

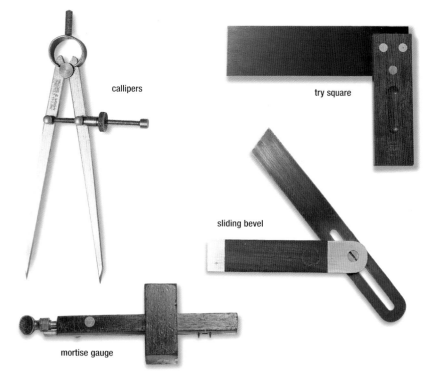

callipers

try square

sliding bevel

mortise gauge

A sliding bevel is a tool used for marking angles on to a square piece of wood. It can be adjusted to any angle, and is especially useful if the angles are to be repeated, such as when setting out treads for a staircase.

A good alternative for marking frequently repeated angles, such as on a staircase, is to make up a jig or template that can be laid on to the stringer (the long diagonal part of the staircase) and mark the treads accordingly. You should be able to buy such templates from most professional workshops. They are available in hardboard and Perspex.

ABOVE: Use a try square for marking right-angles. Keep it clean and make sure the blade is not loose. It can be used with a pencil or a marking knife as required.

THE RIGHT MARKER

Use a carpenter's pencil, ordinary pencil or chinagraph for setting out measurements. Never use a magic marker or a ballpoint pen, since the marks are virtually impossible to remove and will spoil your work. Whichever marking tool you choose, keep it sharp to ensure accuracy.

ABOVE: Use a mortise gauge to scribe directly on to the wood. The two steel pins of the tool are independently adjustable on accurate brass slides, while the sliding stock runs against the face of the work. There may be a single pin on the opposite side for marking a scribed line, used to gauge thickness.

PLANES

The most commonly used varieties of plane are the jack plane for flattening the faces and edges of boards, and the smoothing plane for fine finishing. Good-quality examples are sufficiently weighty to avoid "chatter", which occurs when the plane skips over the surface of the wood without cutting properly. A block plane is often used for planing end grain because its blade is set at a low angle that severs the wood fibres cleanly.

block
plane

smoothing
plane

jack
plane

PLANING TECHNIQUE

Body weight plays a large part in planing technique. Position your body with your hips and shoulders in line with the plane, and your feet spaced apart.

At the beginning of the stroke, apply pressure to the front handle of the plane, switching to a general downward pressure during the middle of the stroke, and finish off by applying most of the pressure to the back of the plane at the end of the board.

PLANING END GRAIN AND BOARDS

Plane end grain and boards using a block plane. To avoid splitting the ends of the wood, work from each side toward the middle. A useful technique for planing wide boards is to work diagonally, or even at right angles, across the grain. This method will remove material efficiently. To finish, it will be necessary to make fine cuts with the grain to obtain a smooth surface. Run your fingers lightly over the surface to identify any unevenness that needs removing.

TIPS

• Cheap planes often serve to blunt enthusiasm by poor performance. Always buy the best you can afford and keep them sharp.
• Check for sharpness and adjustment each time a plane is used – and make sure the wood to be planed is held firmly.

STARTING TO PLANE

1 The correct body position helps to achieve the desired result. Keep your hips and shoulders parallel to the direction in which you are planing, with your weight balanced on both feet.

2 Apply pressure to the front of the plane as you begin the stroke, equal pressure to front and back in the middle of the stroke, and pressure on the back of the plane at the end of the stroke.

3 When planing a narrow edge, make sure you keep the plane centralized to ensure an even cut. To do this, you can tuck your fingers under the sole plate as a guide.

4 If you have identical edges to plane, clamp them together and work on both at once. Check from time to time that you are planing them square with the aid of a try square.

POWER PLANERS

If you need to remove large amounts of wood, a power planer is very useful. An electric planer should be handled with great care as it is extremely easy to remove too much wood and ruin the work. The depth of cut in one pass ranges from 1.5 to 5mm ($\frac{1}{16}$ to $\frac{3}{16}$in) on more powerful models; 3mm ($\frac{1}{8}$in) is quite adequate for most general purposes.

Look for a model that offers a dust bag to collect the copious shavings produced. Tungsten-carbide-tipped (TCT) disposable blades are best when working with manufactured boards such as MDF (medium-density fiberboard) and plywood.

The cutter block, in which the blades are mounted, rotates at very high speed and should be treated with great respect. Always hold the tool with both hands and keep it moving so that it does not cut for too long in one spot.

Although the power planer is very fast, the hand-held version rarely gives the quality of finish that can be achieved with a well-set and sharpened bench plane. Unless you intend doing a lot of work where a power planer will be needed, you may find it less expensive to hire one when you require it. Most tool hirers will have them.

power planer

ABOVE: Use two hands to plane end grain with a power planer to ensure complete control.

ABOVE: Plane across wide boards with a power planer to give quick results.

POWER PLANING TECHNIQUES

It is very important to hold a power planer with both hands, as it can be a very aggressive tool. Make sure that the flex (power cord) is well out of the way so that it does not impede the work.

Keep your hands well away from the blades and wait for the cutter block to stop spinning before putting the tool down on the workbench.

Check for sharpness and adjustment each time you use a power planer, and make sure the wood to be planed is held firmly in a vice or clamped down.

As with the hand plane, an electric planer can also be used across the grain of wide boards for quick results, provided that final finishing is with the grain.

1 The depth of cut is controlled by the rotary knob at the front, which doubles as a handle. Push down firmly and evenly on the machine to remove a constant thickness of stock in one pass. The side fence keeps the sole plate square to the edge.

2 Most planers have a V-groove machined in the bottom of the sole plate to permit chamfering. Locate the groove on the square edge of the work to position the cutters at 45 degrees to each adjoining face. The work is in a jig to hold it in position.

3 Some models allow you to form rebates (rabbets) up to 25mm (1in) deep, using the side fence to control the rebate width. The design of the planer body dictates the maximum rebate capacity, so always check that the tool you buy meets your needs.

CHISELS

Each with its own specific use, chisels come in a variety of shapes and sizes. For jobs around the home, only three basic types are required. Most commonly used is the firmer chisel, which is a compromise between a mortise chisel and a bevel-edged chisel. It can be regarded as a general-purpose tool, having a strong blade of rectangular section designed for medium/heavy work. Most home woodworkers will find blade widths of 6mm (¼in), 12mm (½in), 19mm (¾in) and 25mm (1in) sufficient for their needs.

SPECIAL-PURPOSE CHISELS

Bevel-edged chisels have thinner blades than firmer chisels. The tops of the blades are bevelled along their length to allow better access into small recesses and corners, and to permit fine slicing cuts to be made in the wood.

The mortise chisel is a sturdy tool with a lot of steel just below the handle. It is used for chopping deep mortises across the grain, so it has to be able to withstand blows from a heavy mallet. For this reason, a wooden-handled mortise chisel may have a metal band around the top of the handle to prevent it from splitting. The thickness of the steel blade also allows it to be used as a lever for cleaning the waste from the mortise.

Many new chisels have shatter-resistant polypropylene handles that can be struck with a mallet, or even a hammer, without damage since the material is virtually unbreakable.

TIPS

• Always make sure your chisels are sharp. A blunt tool needs more pressure to force it through the work and is more likely to slip, possibly causing an accident.
• Do not leave chisels lying where the blades can touch metal objects. Fit them with blade guards or keep them in a cloth.

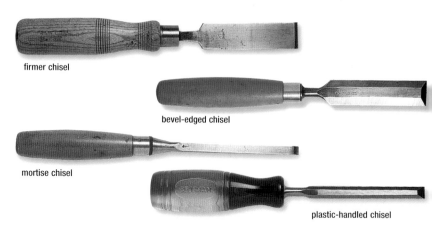

firmer chisel

bevel-edged chisel

mortise chisel

plastic-handled chisel

CHISELLING TECHNIQUES

Always aim to remove as much waste wood as possible from the cut before using the chisel. For example, remove the waste with a saw before cleaning up with a chisel or, when cutting a mortise, drill out the waste and use the chisel to clean and square-up the sides.

When using a router to cut slots and rebates (rabbets), square the ends by hand with a chisel.

Remember to cut away from the marked line when chiselling so that any splitting will occur in the waste wood, and always cut away from yourself to avoid injury. Work patiently and never be tempted to make cuts that are too large. The chisel should be pushed or struck with one hand while being guided with the other.

HORIZONTAL PARING

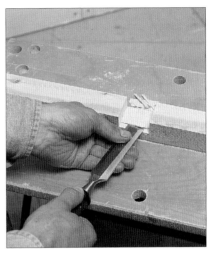

1 Horizontal paring, working from both sides to the middle, prevents "break out" and results in clean work using less pressure.

2 Chamfer an edge, first using the chisel with the bevel down to remove most of the waste. Then make the finishing cuts with the blade held bevel up, taking fine parings.

3 When making the finished cuts, use your thumb to control the cutting edge of the chisel, holding it close to the end of the blade. Make sure the chisel is sharp.

VERTICAL PARING

ABOVE: When paring vertically by hand, guide the chisel blade with one hand while pushing down firmly on the handle with the other.

REMOVING LARGE AMOUNTS

ABOVE: To remove larger amounts of waste wood, hold the chisel vertically and strike the handle firmly with a wooden mallet.

MORTISING

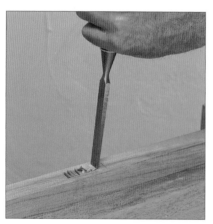

ABOVE: You can form a mortise completely with a chisel, but it is much quicker to remove most of the waste by drilling it out, then use a chisel to clean up the sides and ends of the cutout.

DOVETAILS

ABOVE: Dovetail joints are common in cabinet work. Begin by removing the bulk of the waste with a coping saw before using a narrow, bevel-edged chisel to finish off.

SHARPENING EQUIPMENT

A good sharpening stone is a vital part of the tool kit. Without a sharp edge, a chisel will be not only difficult to work with, but also dangerous. The chisel will follow where the wood directs it, rather than where you want it to go, and can easily slip.

Chisels should be sharpened at the beginning and end of every session. If they are attended to regularly, just a few minutes' work will keep the honed edges in prime condition. Once in a while, a longer honing session might be necessary – if the bevel loses its original angle or if the edge is chipped.

Natural sharpening stones are quite expensive, and synthetic versions are commonly used. Japanese water stones are of natural stone and need water as a lubricant. They can produce a finely ground edge on the best-quality steel. For more general use, however, oilstones are sufficient.

A combination stone is the best buy, two stones of different grades being bonded together back to back.

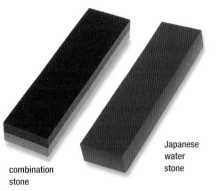

combination stone

Japanese water stone

SHARPENING PLANE IRONS

To sharpen a plane iron, apply a coat of thin oil to the oilstone, hold the blade at 35 degrees to the stone and maintain this angle while working it backward and forward. Honing jigs, which set the angle exactly, are readily available. Lay the back of the iron flat on the oilstone and rub off the burr formed by the sharpening process. Clean out the inside of the plane before reassembly, and apply a drop of oil to the adjustment mechanism.

1 Hold the iron at a steady angle while rubbing it on the oilstone.

2 Remove the burr from a sharpened blade by rubbing the back flat on the stone.

SAWS

The most common saw used by the do-it-yourselfer is the hand saw. This is used for cross-cutting (across the grain) and ripping (along the grain), and the teeth of the saw are set accordingly, so you will need to ask your tool supplier for the correct one. There are also general-purpose hand saws that are reasonably suited to both tasks. These are quite often hardpoint saws, which cannot be sharpened, but their specially hardened teeth give them a long life.

The tenon saw, sometimes called a backsaw because of the solid strengthening bar along its top edge, is made specifically for cutting the tenons of mortise-and-tenon joints and other fine work. Really fine work is done with a dovetail saw, which is similar to a tenon saw, but has more teeth to the inch to give a finer cut.

The tenon saw is often used with a bench hook for making cross-cuts in small pieces, and one can be made quite easily as a do-it-yourself project. They usually measure about 300 x 150mm (12 x 6in). The mitre box is another handy aid for use with a tenon saw, allowing 90- and 45-degree angles to be cut accurately, but the beginner is best advised to buy one rather than attempt to make one.

A mitre saw makes short work of cutting accurate angles and offers fine adjustment. It is well worth the investment if working with delicate mouldings or making picture frames.

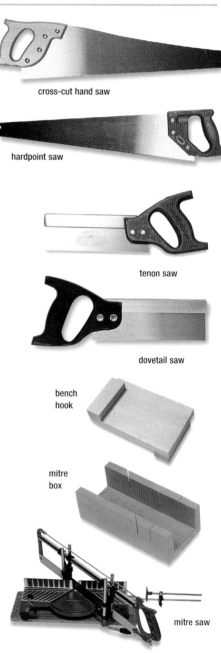

cross-cut hand saw

hardpoint saw

tenon saw

dovetail saw

bench hook

mitre box

mitre saw

SAWING TECHNIQUES

When beginning a cut with a hand saw, draw the saw back toward your body to sever the wood fibres and produce a small kerf – the groove in which the saw blade will run. Always cut on the waste side of the marked line for perfect results.

When using a mitre box to make an angled cut, begin with the back of the saw raised slightly. This will make the cut easier to start.

TIP

Always find a comfortable position in which to saw. It will produce better results and reduce the risks of back strain or other injury.

ABOVE: Draw the saw back a few times to start the cut, using your thumb to support the blade until a kerf has formed.

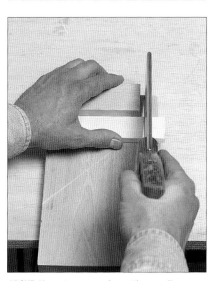

ABOVE: Use a tenon saw for cutting small components or sawing tenons and the like. A bench hook aids the cross-cutting.

ABOVE: A standard mitre box permits 90- and 45-degree angled cuts to be made with a tenon saw for a variety of applications.

POWER SAWS

Invaluable for saving a lot of time and hard work, a power saw can also do a lot of damage if used incorrectly. Never force a saw through the work.

If the blade is not sharp, or the motor is underpowered, not only will the cut be inaccurate, but also you'll be putting your safety at risk. Let the saw do the work, guiding it slowly, but surely, along the line. Use an adjustable fence if possible when making straight parallel cuts.

circular saw

CIRCULAR SAWS

A hand-held circular saw can be used for both cross-cutting and ripping, and many are supplied with a dual-purpose, tungsten-carbide-tipped blade for a long life. It is almost a necessity for the home woodworker and is an excellent investment; there are many quite inexpensive and reliable brands.

CIRCULAR SAW BLADES

Check that the bore of the blade (the diameter of the central hole that fits over the spindle) is compatible with the machine, as different makes vary. As with hand saws, the type of blade should suit the material and the cutting action, whether ripping along the grain, cross-cutting, or making fine cuts in veneered or laminated panels. Carbide teeth are cheaper for most general-purpose work; tungsten-carbide-tipped blades are sharper and much harder wearing. The latter should be used when cutting composite materials and manufactured boards such as plywood and MDF (medium-density fiberboard).

ABOVE: A circular saw will make light work of cutting wood, but be sure not to overload it, and always have the guards in place. Use a good-quality hand saw for smaller jobs.

JIGSAWS

Another very handy tool is the jigsaw (saber saw). It is suitable for both straight and curved cuts, saving a lot of hard work.

jigsaw

Most jigsaws come into their own when cutting out curved shapes from manufactured boards, such as MDF (medium-density fiberboard) and plywood.

If large amounts of curved or shaped work are envisaged, a small bandsaw is a useful addition to the workshop. These can be inexpensive. Fret/scroll saws are very similar to jigsaws, being fitted with a reciprocating movement. They are used for fine pierced and detail work, and are capable of turning out very delicate results.

ABOVE: A jigsaw (saber saw) is very good for making curved cuts. Most have adjustable cutting angles. Be sure your work is securely clamped to keep it firmly in place.

JIGSAW BLADES

Jigsaw (saber saw) blades are made for many purposes, but check that the model of jigsaw you buy will accept standard-fitting blades. Many specialized blades are available for cutting all kinds of material, such as wood, manufactured boards, metal, ceramics, plastics and laminates. A knife blade has no teeth, and is designed for cutting leather and rubber sheeting. Bi-metal blades, although more expensive, will last longer and are less inclined to bend. Most blades are 100mm (4in) long, allowing a depth of cut of 50–65mm (2–2½in), but heavy-duty blades are available up to 150mm (6in) long. These should only be fitted to a machine with a powerful motor designed to accept the extra load.

KNIVES

The do-it-yourself enthusiast will need a variety of knives, some of which have very specific functions. Some do not actually conform to the conventional idea of a knife at all, but all have metal blades and are essentially cutting tools.

MARKING KNIVES

The purpose of a marking knife is to mark a sawing line, by lightly cutting the surface wood fibres, and assist in the beginning of a saw cut. Not only does this provide a permanent guide line, but it also prevents the fibres from splintering as the saw cuts through. These tools are usually about 200mm (8in) long and make a much finer line than a pencil.

They are normally used in conjunction with a steel rule, straightedge or try square and are bevelled on one side only so that they can be used tightly against the steel edge for accuracy. They are available in both left- and right-handed versions.

Marking knives without pointed ends are also frequently used, and these are bevelled on either the left- or right-hand side, depending on the needs of the user.

Twin-bladed knives are available and are adjusted by a set screw and locking knob. Typically, the blades can be set to a spacing of 3–19mm ($\frac{1}{8}$–$\frac{3}{4}$in). This type of knife is used for marking parallel lines, gauging mortises and cutting thin strips from veneers for decorative inlay work.

GENERAL-PURPOSE KNIVES

By far the most common and useful general-purpose knife is the craft knife, which has a store of replacement blades in the handle. This is an indispensable tool which can be used for many purposes.

Another very handy tool is the scalpel. More delicate and invasive than the craft knife, a scalpel is ideal for cutting out templates and particularly useful for cleaning up deeply indented

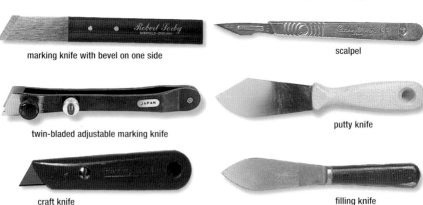

marking knife with bevel on one side

scalpel

twin-bladed adjustable marking knife

putty knife

craft knife

filling knife

MARKING OUT

ABOVE: Mark a line across the grain with the knife held firmly against the steel edge of a try square. This gives a very fine line of severed wood fibres, which is ideal to work to with either a saw or a chisel.

ABOVE: A typical example of a knife being used with a steel rule. Note how the fingers are spread to keep a firm and even downward pressure on the rule, allowing the knife to be used hard against the rule's edge.

cuts in carvings and routed work. Scalpels are made with a variety of handles and have replaceable blades.

MISCELLANEOUS KNIVES

Putty knives often find their way into the do-it-yourselfer's tool kit. They have specially shaped ends to their blades to make "cutting off" easier. This means withdrawing the knife from the work without damaging the soft putty that is being applied to a window pane or moulding, for example.

The filling knife is a familiar decorator's tool with a flexible spring-tempered blade that is ideal for forcing soft material, such as wood filler, into knot

holes, cracks and blemishes in wood, and plaster filler into cracks in walls. These come in a variety of shapes and sizes and are often confused with stripping knives, which have thicker and less flexible blades.

TIPS

• Never use a scalpel or craft knife with excessive pressure. The blade may shatter and sharp pieces fly up into your unprotected eyes.
• Always place the hand not holding the knife behind the blade. This prevents injury if the blade slips.

DRILLS AND BITS

Accurate drilling is an important do-it-yourself technique. It is much easier with a hand-held power drill, and even more so with a bench-mounted pillar drill.

CARPENTER'S BRACE

Drilling by hand with a carpenter's brace still has a place, and a hand drill is useful for smaller jobs, especially in sites far removed from electric power. However, even in these circumstances, the cordless power drill has largely overcome the difficulty of finding a source of electric power.

CORDLESS DRILL/DRIVER

This tool is worth its weight in gold in situations without power, and it is particularly safe near water. It is rechargeable and usually comes with a spare battery. The variable torque and speed settings make it ideal for doubling as a screwdriver. Although generally not as powerful as a mains-powered drill, it is more than

adequate for most jobs. Use it for drilling clearance holes for screws, fitting and removing screws, and drilling holes for dowels.

Heavier work, especially that which involves using flat bits or Forstner bits to remove very large areas of wood, is best undertaken with a mains-powered electric drill to save time and avoid the need for constant recharging of the battery.

VARIETIES OF BIT

Great advances have also been made in the pattern of drill bits. For example, there are bits designed for setting dowels. Dowel jointing is often used in projects built with manufactured boards, such as chipboard (particle board) and plywood, and the bits produce flat-bottomed holes.

cordless drill

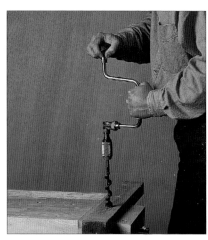

ABOVE: A carpenter's brace is ideal for boring large holes. Its design provides plenty of leverage to turn flat and auger bits.

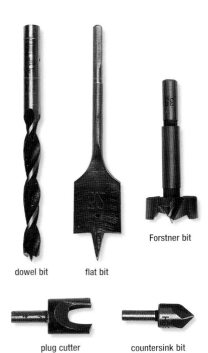

Forstner bit

dowel bit   flat bit

plug cutter   countersink bit

from a piece of scrap wood. Then the plugs are glued into holes in the workpiece to conceal fixing screws. Most cutters come with a special matching bit that bores a screw clearance hole and plug countersink in one operation.

Another common drilling accessory is the countersink bit. This allows the head of a screw to be set flush with the surface of the wood. Again, this is best used in a pillar drill with a depth stop to ensure accuracy.

Forstner bits are designed to drill large, flat-bottomed holes that do not pass through the wood, such as holes that might be needed to accommodate kitchen cabinet hinges. The bits will drill deep holes accurately, even in the end grain of the wood, which is usually very difficult.

There are also flat bits that work with a scraping action, cutting large holes very rapidly, although these are not as accurate as conventional twist bits. The latter are used for making small holes in wood, metal and other rigid materials, but specially hardened types are needed for steel. For the do-it-yourselfer on a limited budget, an adjustable bit is a good investment, but these can only be used in a hand brace.

DRILLING ACCESSORIES

Plug cutters are useful additions to any workshop, especially when quality work is undertaken. The cutter is fitted in a pillar drill and used to remove plugs

ABOVE: Many drill bits can be sharpened with a specialized grinding attachment designed to be run off a hand-held power drill.

ASSEMBLING

Sooner or later, the do-it-yourselfer is likely to be faced with the need to join two or more pieces of a workpiece together. In some cases, this can be done by forming joints and using glue, although some means of clamping the pieces together while the glue dries must be found. Often, however, some form of mechanical fixing is called for. The most commonly used fixings are nails and screws, although occasionally nuts and bolts may be required. There are many types of nail, some of which require special hammers to drive them, while screws have different head designs and need the correct type of screwdriver. Nuts and bolts can be assembled and dismantled with spanners and/or sockets.

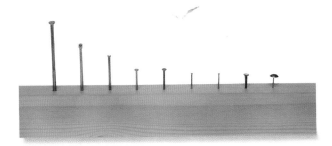

CLAMPS

Many do-it-yourself tasks require two or more sections of a workpiece to be held together temporarily while a more permanent fixing is made, often with glue. A variety of clamps is available for this purpose, many of them with specific uses. Keen woodworkers may make their own clamps (or cramps as they are often called) from scrap wood or other materials.

COMMONLY USED CLAMPS

The most common clamp in the workshop is the G-clamp. This is a general-purpose tool that is available with a variety of throat sizes. It may be used on its own or in conjunction with others when, for example, working on the surface of a wide board or holding boards together for gluing.

The sash clamp was designed specifically for assembling window frames, or sashes, but it is also often used when edge-jointing boards to form large panels for table tops and similar items.

Sometimes, it is useful to be able to apply a clamp with one hand while holding the workpiece in the other, which is when the single-handed clamp comes into its own. It works on a simple ratchet system, rather like a mastic (caulking) gun.

For picture frames and heavier items with 45-degree mitred joints at the corners, there is the mitre clamp. This can be quite a complex affair with screw handles for tightening or a very

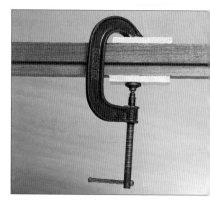

ABOVE: The G-clamp in a typical application. Note the packing pieces beneath the jaws to prevent bruising of the wood.

simple "clothes-peg" (pin) type arrangement, that can be applied to the work very quickly.

SPECIAL-PURPOSE CLAMPS

There are many of these, but one that the do-it-yourself enthusiast may find useful is the cam clamp, which is wooden with cork faces. This is a quickly operated clamp often used by musical instrument makers. Its advantages are its speed in use, its lightness and its simplicity. The cam clamp is ideal for small holding jobs, although it cannot exert a great deal of pressure.

cam clamp

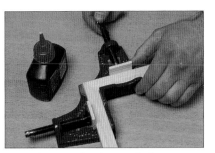

ABOVE: Small wooden picture and mirror frames can be easily assembled with the aid of inexpensive mitre clamps.

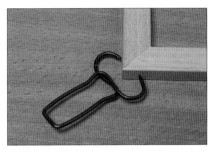

ABOVE: This clever little clamp works by means of spring pressure. It can be applied quickly and easily to small assemblies.

ABOVE: Use sash clamps to edge-joint boards to form a panel such as a table top. Reverse the central clamp to even out the pressure.

ABOVE: Home-made clamps used for the same purpose, but this time the pressure is exerted by means of wedges.

CLAMPS IN USE

Apply pressure to a joint or the assembly you are working on as soon as possible after gluing – make a habit of preparing everything you need in advance. Keep a box of small scraps of wood handy and use them to protect the surface of the work. It is often said that you can never have too many clamps, and you will soon start collecting a selection of different types and sizes to suit all kinds of assembly technique. Many can be home-made.

TIPS

• Do not be tempted to release clamps too quickly. Be patient, allowing plenty of drying time for the glue – overnight at least, or as specified by the maker.
• Think through the sequence for the clamping process and make sure you have enough clamps to hand before you apply any glue. With a complex or large structure, you may decide you need another person to help.

NAILS AND HAMMERS

There is no such thing as an "ordinary" nail. All nails have been derived for specific purposes, although some can be put to several uses. Similarly, various types of hammer are available – always use the correct tool for the job. Wooden-handled hammers have a natural spring in the handles, which makes them easier to control than steel-handled types.

NAILS

The wire nail can be used for many simple tasks, such as box-making, fencing and general carpentry. Lost-head and oval nails are useful where there is no need for a flat head, or when it is desirable for the nails to be concealed, such as when fixing cladding or boards.

Oval nails can be driven below the surface of the work with less likelihood of them splitting the wood. They should be inserted with their heads in line with the grain.

The cut nail is stamped from metal sheet and has a tapering, rectangular section, which gives it excellent holding properties. It is largely used for fixing flooring.

Panel pins (brads), as their name suggests, are used for fixing thin panels and cladding. They are nearly always punched out of sight below the surface, as are veneer pins.

When there is a need to secure thin or fragile sheet material, such as roofing felt or plasterboard (gypsum board), large-headed nails are used. These are commonly called clout nails, but may also be found under specific names, such as roofing nails and plasterboard nails. Their large heads spread the pressure and prevent the materials from tearing or crumbling. They are usually galvanized to protect them against rust when used outdoors. Zinc nails are used for roofing because they are rustproof and easy to cut through when renewing slates.

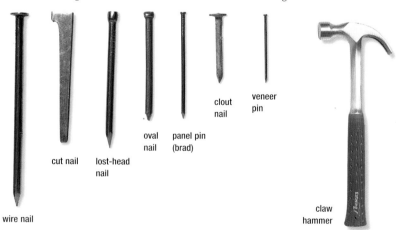

clout nail

veneer pin

oval nail

panel pin (brad)

cut nail

lost-head nail

wire nail

claw hammer

HAMMERS

The essential hammer for the do-it-yourselfer is the claw hammer, the claw being used to extract nails. About 365–450g (13–16oz) is a good weight to aim for, since the hammer should be heavy enough to drive large nails. It is a mistake to use a hammer that is too light, as this tends to bend the nails rather than drive them.

For lighter nails, a cross-pein or Warrington hammer is useful, since the flat head can be used to start the nail or pin without risk of hitting your fingers. For even smaller panel pins, the pin hammer is used.

CARPENTER'S MALLET

It should be remembered that the carpenter's mallet, often made from solid beech, is a form of hammer, but it should never be used for striking anything other than wood or similar soft materials, otherwise serious damage will result.

DOVETAIL NAILING

Cross, or dovetail, nailing is a simple and useful method of holding a butt joint strongly in end grain. When several nails are being driven into one piece of wood, avoid putting them in straight; slanting them will help prevent splitting.

ABOVE: The claw hammer's ability to extract as well as drive nails makes it a useful tool for do-it-yourself projects.

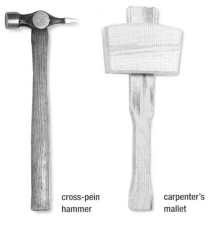

cross-pein hammer

carpenter's mallet

SCREWS AND SCREWDRIVERS

The holding power of screws is much greater than that of nails, and screwed work can easily be taken apart again without damage to any of the components, unless of course it is also glued. Driving screws does take longer than nailing and they are more expensive, but they will give the appearance of quality and craftsmanship to most work.

TYPES OF SCREW

The most common wood screws may be made of mild steel or brass, often with countersunk heads that may be flat or raised. There are many different plated finishes available, ranging from chrome, used for internal fixings such as mirrors, to zinc, which will resist rust.

Brass screws will not rust at all and are often used in woods such as oak, where steel would cause blue staining due to the tannic acid in the sap.

HEAD PATTERNS AND SCREW SIZES

There are various types of screw head used for both hand and power driving. The most common is the slot-head screw, followed by the Phillips head and the Pozidriv, both of which have a cruciform pattern in the head to take the screwdriver blade.

Screw sizes are complex, combining the length and the diameter (gauge): for example, "inch-and-a-half eight" describes a screw that is 1½in (40mm) long and gauge 8.

TYPES OF SCREWDRIVER

For woodworking, the traditional hand screwdriver has an oval wooden handle and is used to drive slot-head screws only. It is available in a variety of sizes. A range of plastic-handled tools of

flat and raised countersunk screws

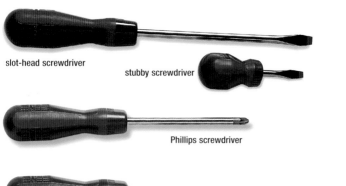

slot-head screwdriver

stubby screwdriver

Phillips screwdriver

Pozidriv screwdriver

slotted screw head

Phillips screw head

Pozidriv screw head

various sizes is also available, designed to drive Phillips and Pozidriv screws, as well as slot-heads.

A recent innovation is the screwdriver bit set, containing a handle and a number of interchangeable tips to fit various screw types and sizes.

Power screwdrivers and drill/drivers vastly increase the rate of work. They can offer various torque settings that allow the screw heads to be set just flush with the work surface. Power drivers are also very useful for dismantling screwed joints and furniture because they will run in reverse.

Keeping the head of a slot-head screwdriver correctly ground to prevent it from slipping is very important. Remember also that the blade width must equal the length of the screw slot for the greatest efficiency and to prevent both slipping and damage to the screw head. Always use the correct size of screwdriver with Phillips and Pozidriv screws, otherwise both the screw head and the screwdriver are likely to be damaged.

cordless
electric
drill/driver

USING SCREWS

Driving a screw is a more skilled task than nailing. It is usually advisable to drill pilot holes first to ease the screws' passage through the wood and to ensure that they go in straight. In hardwoods, pre-drilling is vital, otherwise the screws will shear off when pressure is exerted by the screwdriver. Brass screws are particularly soft, so steel screws of the same size should be inserted to pre-cut the threads.

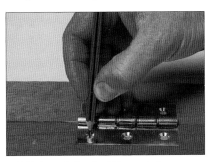

ABOVE: Screw holes should be marked very carefully when fitting hinges.

ABOVE: Where possible, use the screwdriver with both hands to prevent slipping.

PINCERS AND PLIERS

Every do-it-yourself enthusiast's tool kit should include a range of hand tools for gripping small items. Chief among these are pincers, used for removing nails and similar fixings, and general-purpose combination pliers, which offer a variety of gripping and cutting features.

PINCERS

A good pair of pincers will remove nails and tacks with little trouble. The rolling action required to remove a nail with pincers is very similar to that used with a claw hammer. An ideal length is about 175mm (7in) to ensure good leverage, which is essential. The jaws should touch along their entire width and be properly aligned to provide maximum grip.

It is important that pincers do not damage the work, and for this reason, broad jaws – about 25mm (1in) wide – that will spread the load are best.

Some pincers come with a handy tack lifter at the end of one of the handles. Purpose-made tack lifters are very useful for upholstery work, and if you intend doing any furniture making or restoration, it is well worth investing in such a tool.

Another special tack and nail remover is the nail puller, or "cat's-paw", as it is sometimes known. This tool has a standard tack remover at one end and a large, right-angled claw at the other for getting under the heads of stubborn nails. The claw can be tapped under the head of an embedded nail with a small hammer.

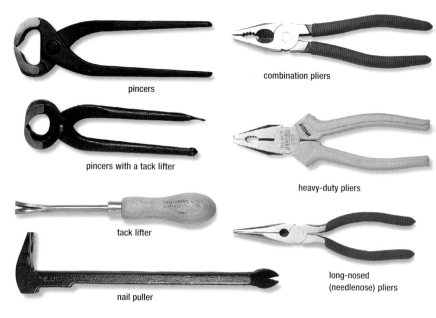

pincers

combination pliers

pincers with a tack lifter

heavy-duty pliers

tack lifter

long-nosed
(needlenose) pliers

nail puller

PLIERS

These come in a bewildering range of types and sizes, many of which have very specific uses.

Combination pliers and heavy-duty pliers are used for gripping, twisting and cutting. They come in various sizes, but a good pair would be about 200mm (8in) long and probably have plastic or rubber handle grips for comfort and to provide insulation against electric shock.

Long-nosed (needlenose) pliers are rather more specialized and are used for gripping small objects in confined spaces. Some have cranked jaws at various angles for access to awkward places. They come in many sizes.

ABOVE: When using pincers to remove a nail, protect the wood by slipping a piece of hardboard or plywood below the pincer head.

ABOVE: Remove tacks from wood with a tack lifter. Protect the surface with hardboard or a piece of plywood.

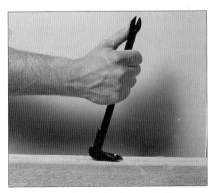

ABOVE: The flat behind the claw of this Japanese nail puller can be tapped with a hammer to drive the claw under the nail head.

ABOVE: When using pliers, hold them firmly, keeping your palm away from the pivot, which can pinch your skin as the jaws close.

SPANNERS AND WRENCHES

Although spanners and wrenches may be thought of as tools for the garage, there are many do-it-yourself tasks that require these gripping and twisting tools, particularly in the kitchen and bathroom, where you are likely to come into contact with pipes and their fittings. All home workshops need at least one comprehensive set of sockets or spanners.

SPANNERS

These are necessary in the home workshop where power tools and machinery are involved. They are needed for changing the blades on circular saws, for adjusting and setting bandsaw guides, and for assembling all manner of machinery stands, tool racks and benches.

A good selection of spanners would include open-ended, ring and combination spanners. These are usually purchased in sets; other tools are bought singly.

It is essential to use a spanner that fits a nut or bolt perfectly, otherwise the fixing will be damaged and you run the risk of skinned knuckles. Spanners are

LEFT: Socket sets are extremely useful and offer a choice of types of drive (such as bars and ratchets) as well as sockets in a variety of sizes.

graduated in specific sizes – metric, Whitworth and A/F are the most common. Open-ended spanners are the most usual. Some have jaws that are offset by about 15 degrees to allow them to contact different flats of nuts when working in tight spots.

Ring spanners have enclosed heads that give a more secure grip. They may have six or 12 points, and can be used on square and hexagonal nuts and bolts. The 12-point version needs only a very small movement for it to contact new

open-ended spanner

ring spanner

combination spanner

adjustable spanner

flats on the nut or bolt head, so it is very useful where there is limited room for movement.

Sockets grip in the same manner as a ring spanner, but are designed to fit a variety of drive handles, of which the ratchet handle is the most useful. This enables the user to continue to turn a nut or bolt without having to remove the socket after each turn. Some large sets offer metric, Whitworth, BSF and A/F sizes. Small sets of additional sockets are available to complement your existing set, allowing you to build up a kit that meets your needs exactly.

WRENCHES

Adjustable spanners and wrenches enable the user to grip various sizes and types of fitting. Some are designed for specific purposes, while others are suitable for more general use.

Basic plumbing tools include adjustable pipe wrenches (known as Stilsons), an adjustable basin wrench and a double-ended basin wrench, both of which will reach up behind a basin to allow removal of the nuts holding taps in place, and water-pump pliers with soft jaws.

Normally, the adjustable spanner is made from forged alloy steel. Self-grip wrenches, or vice grips, can be adjusted to fit pipework or a nut or bolt head, and then can be locked to grip tightly. They are very versatile and useful tools. Water-pump pliers offer five or six settings by virtue of having an adjustable bottom jaw. They are capable of exerting a heavy pressure because of their long handles.

Another variation is the strap wrench, made of a soft pliable material. It is used for gripping container lids.

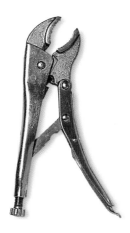

Stilson wrench

self-grip wrench

ABOVE: A strap wrench offers a soft pliable grip that can be used for opening containers.

TIP

Never use a wrench on a nut or bolt if a spanner of the correct size is available. Wrenches are essentially for pipe work and will damage the corners of nuts and bolt heads very quickly. Use the correct tool wherever possible.

FINISHING

No matter what type of finish you apply to a surface, in practically all cases, the smoother the surface, the better the finish. A primary method of achieving smoothness is by sanding with abrasive paper, which can be done by hand or by machine. Paint is the most common finish for a variety of surfaces in the home, and you will need a selection of brushes and rollers to apply it. An alternative to paint is wallpaper – there is no limit to the versatility of modern wallpapers, which can be used for decorating both walls and ceilings. A few specialized tools are needed to do the job. Tiles are a good means of providing a durable, waterproof surface to walls and floors. They require skill to lay, but this is not beyond the average do-it-yourselfer.

SANDERS

Although the term "sanding" is generally used for do-it-yourself projects, it is something of a misnomer. A truer description would be "abrading", because what we call "sandpaper" is, in fact, "glasspaper". In addition, we also use garnet paper, and silicon-carbide and aluminium-oxide abrasive papers, all of which shape wood very efficiently.

GRIT SIZE

One thing abrasive papers all have in common is classification by grit size, and the golden rule is to work progressively down through the grit sizes, from coarse to fine, when smoothing a piece of work. For example, 400 grit is finer than 200 grit and should be employed later in the finishing process. Abrasives can be used by hand or with a variety of machines, both hand-held and stationary. Sanders are also suitable for shaping work, using coarse abrasives for rapid material removal.

TYPES OF SANDER

A tool commonly used for heavy-duty shaping and sanding is the belt sander. This normally has a 75mm (3in) wide belt, running continuously over two rollers, and a dust collection facility.

A belt and disc sander is an inexpensive alternative. It is used for shaping and trimming rather than smoothing, as the piece of work is taken to them.

Many do-it-yourselfers are likely to own an orbital sander, which is useful for general light sanding work such as finishing boards. These sanders are designed to accept either half or a third of a standard-size abrasive sheet and quite often have dedicated sheets made for them. Random orbital sanders are similar, but may employ self-adhesive abrasive sheets that are easy to fit. They can be small enough to be used with one hand in tight spots, but still give a good finish.

HAND SANDING

Always wrap abrasive paper around a cork or rubber block when sanding flat surfaces. Clear the dust away as you work to avoid clogging the paper, particularly on resinous and oily wood. To finish off a rounded edge, wrap a square of paper around a section of moulded wood with the correct profile for the job.

belt sander   orbital sander   random orbital sander

ABOVE: You should hold a belt sander with both hands to prevent it from running away.

ABOVE: The belt sander can be inverted and secured in a woodworking vice.

ABOVE: Belt and disc sanders are used for shaping and trimming, and can be aggressive.

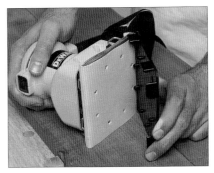

ABOVE: The orbital sander is less ferocious than the belt sander and is easy to control.

MAKING A SANDING BLOCK

1 Fold your sheet of abrasive paper to size and tear it along a sharp edge.

2 Wrap the paper around a cork or rubber block before starting to sand.

PAINTING TOOLS

This is one aspect of do-it-yourself work where you cannot afford to skimp on materials. You will not achieve professional results by using cheap brushes that shed their bristles as you work, or cut-price rollers that disintegrate before the job is finished. Invest in the best quality equipment your budget allows.

CHOOSING BRUSHES

Paintbrushes come in pure bristle, synthetic fibre and even foam versions. The last guarantees that you will not be left with brush strokes, and they are inexpensive enough to discard when you have finished. All natural brushes shed a few bristles in use, but cheap brushes are the worst offenders. Usually, these have fewer bristles to start with and they are often poorly secured. Regard pure bristle brushes as an investment; you can use them repeatedly, and many painters claim that they improve with age.

Synthetic brushes, usually with nylon bristles, have the advantage of being moult-free, and they perform well with water-based paints. A more expensive version, made of polyester and nylon, is particularly easy to handle and said to give a superior finish.

paintbrushes ranging from 100–25mm (4–1in)

cutting-in
(sash) brush

special-effects brushes

foam brush

roller sleeves

roller handle

paint
pads

radiator brush

TOOL BOX ESSENTIALS

Serious painters will need a range of brushes: slimline, 12 and 25mm (½ and 1in), for fiddly areas such as window frames; medium-sized versions, 50 and 75mm (2 and 3in), for doors, floors and skirtings (baseboards); and large types, 100mm (4in), for quick coverage of walls and ceilings. You might like to add a few extras to this basic kit:

• A cutting-in (sash) brush, specially angled to cope with hard-to-reach areas, is particularly useful if you are painting around window frames.

• Special-effects brushes allow you to create distinctive looks such as woodgrain and marbling.

• A radiator brush is designed to reach the wall behind a radiator.

PAINT PADS

If you are new to decorating, you may find that a paint pad is easier to handle than a brush. It gives a speedy and even finish, is light to handle and works well with acrylic paints.

Each pad consists of a layer of fibre on top of a layer of foam, attached to a plastic handle. Use paint pads with a paint tray. If you purchase a kit, a tray will usually be provided.

THE RIGHT ROLLER

If speed is of the essence, a paint roller will be an indispensable part of your decorating tool kit. Once you have a roller, you can simply buy replacement sleeves that fit its existing handle.

Power rollers are mains- or battery-operated and, in theory, they can simplify the whole process, with the paint contained in a portable reservoir. Their disadvantage, however, is that they can result in drips and streaks.

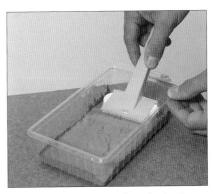

ABOVE: Load paint on to a paint pad using the tray supplied with it.

ABOVE: A power roller will make painting large areas easier, but watch for drips.

WALLPAPERING TOOLS

Using the correct tools will make the job of hanging wallpaper much easier, allowing you to achieve a more professional finish. Some are needed specifically for wallpapering; others are likely to be part of your standard do-it-yourself tool kit. When buying decorating tools, opt for quality rather than quantity.

MEASURING AND MARKING

A retractable steel tape is essential for taking measurements, while a long metal straightedge, a spirit (carpenter's) level or plumbline and a pencil will be needed for marking levels, vertical guidelines on walls and the positions of fixtures.

CUTTING AND TRIMMING

For cutting wallpaper to length and trimming edges, you will need a pair of paperhanger's scissors, which have

long blades and curved tips used for creasing paper into angles. Choose scissors that are at least 250mm (10in) long and made from stainless steel, or which have been specially coated so that they will not rust.

A sharp craft knife can also be used for trimming and will be easier to use with vinyl wallcoverings. Various trimming tools are also available, including the roller cutter, which enables you to crease and cut into edges with a single movement, and is accurate and simple to use.

PASTING

For mixing and applying paste, you will need a plastic bucket and a paste brush. Proper paste brushes have synthetic bristles and will be easier to clean than ordinary paintbrushes. A pasting table is not essential, but

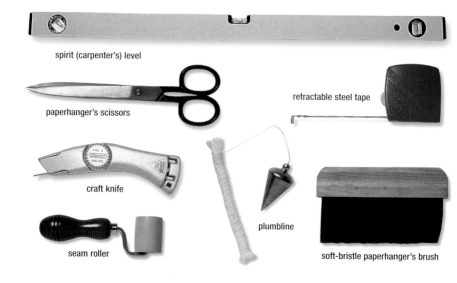

spirit (carpenter's) level

paperhanger's scissors

retractable steel tape

craft knife

plumbline

seam roller

soft-bristle paperhanger's brush

is extremely useful. They are also inexpensive and fold for easy storage. For ready-pasted wallcoverings, a polystyrene soaking trough is required.

SAFE ACCESS

Hanging wallpaper may also involve working at heights, so safe access equipment will be required. A set of sturdy steps will be suitable for papering walls, but a safe platform will be needed for access to ceilings and stairwells.

FINISHING

A paperhanger's brush is the best tool for smoothing down wallpaper, although a sponge can be used for vinyl wallcoverings. For the best results, choose a brush with soft, flexible bristles and buy the largest size that you can manage comfortably. Do not use wallpaper brushes with a metal ferrule or collar on them for this job, as you might inadvertently tear or mark delicate wallcoverings.

Use a cellulose decorator's sponge rather than an ordinary household sponge. This type of sponge is made of a higher-density material, which is firmer and will hold water better.

A seam roller will give a neat finish to joints and the edges of borders, but should not be used on wallpaper with an embossed pattern. Types made from wood and plastic are available. A soft plastic seam roller is the best option as it is less likely to leave marks on thin or overpasted wallpapers.

ABOVE: For smooth wall coverings, a seam roller can be used to make sure that the seams are well bonded to the wall. Do not use a seam roller on textured or embossed wall coverings, though, as it will flatten the embossing.

AVOIDING PASTE DRIPS

A length of string tied tightly across the top of a wallpaper paste bucket makes a handy brush rest. Use the string rather than the side of the bucket for removing excess adhesive from the pasting brush.

TILING TOOLS

Even the simplest of ceramic tiling jobs will require a small selection of specialized tools, while a major project requires quite a few. In addition, you will have to call on tools from your normal do-it-yourself tool kit, such as a retractable steel tape, a straightedge, spirit (carpenter's) level, a saw and a hammer. You will also need to make a tiling gauge, for setting out the rows of tiles. This should be a wooden batten, 1.2m (4ft) long, marked off in tile widths (with an allowance for the joints between).

ADHESIVE AND GROUTING TOOLS

Apply adhesive to the wall with a small pointing trowel, then create a series of ridges in it with a notched spreader. This allows the adhesive to spread when the tile is pressed home, ensuring an even thickness.

Tile spacers are required when using standard field tiles to provide a uniform grouting gap between them. Other types of tile have bevelled edges that create a grouting gap automatically when butted together.

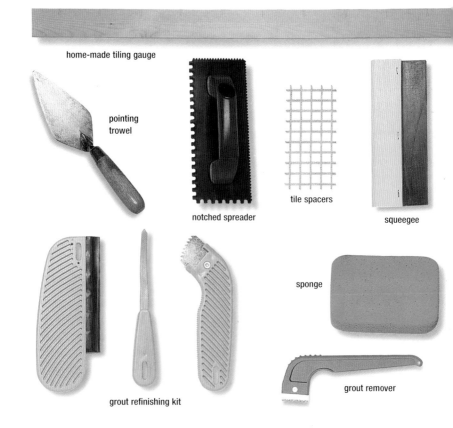

home-made tiling gauge

pointing trowel

notched spreader

tile spacers

squeegee

grout refinishing kit

sponge

grout remover

A squeegee will be needed at the grouting stage to force grout into the gaps between tiles, while a grout finisher will provide the joints with a neat profile. If you don't have a grout finisher, you can substitute it with a short length of wooden dowel. Wipe off excess adhesive from the tiles with a sponge.

Various tools are available for removing old grout when carrying out repairs or renovation work. Take care when using them not to chip the edges of the tiles.

CUTTING AND SHAPING TOOLS

Straight cuts can be made with a simple tile scorer, straightedge and tile snapper, but an all-in-one tile cutter or tile jig will make life easier for the beginner. Most incorporate a measuring device, trimmer and snapping mechanism in one unit.

Tile nippers can be used for cutting off small pieces of tile, while a tile saw is good for cutting out complex shapes. Once a tile has been cut, you can smooth its edges with a tile file.

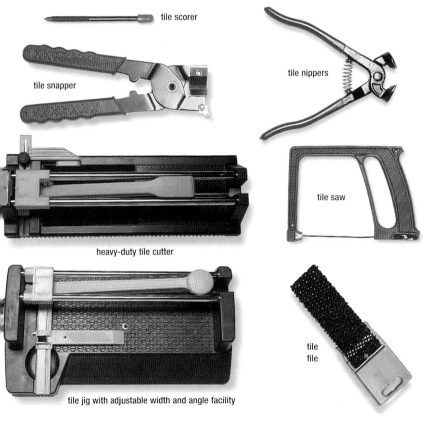

tile scorer

tile snapper

tile nippers

heavy-duty tile cutter

tile saw

tile file

tile jig with adjustable width and angle facility

INDEX

The publisher would like to thank
the following manufacturers
for supplying pictures: Axminster
38bl; Black and Decker 28t.

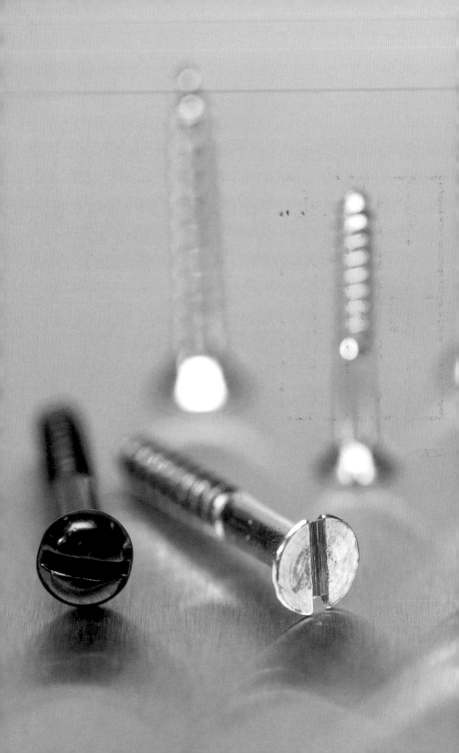